Everyday
Prayers
for
Children

Your Guide for talking to God

Written by

Funke Ogunoiki

This book belongs to

....

First Published in the United Kingdom in 2021

A CIP catalogue record for this book is available from the British Library.

ISBN: 979 8 589409 85 7

The author can be contacted via email at TrulyMakingADifference@gmail.com

To God the Father, the Son and the Holy Spirit, to You be the Glory, Honour and Adoration

Acknowledgements

With special thanks to my husband, Dr Adebola Ogunoiki, for supporting me with the writing of this book and his help in caring for the children while I wrote this book.

Contents

A Note From The Author

I grew up in a Christian home, attended Sunday School as a child and at the age of 15, I developed an interest in working with children with the aim of making a difference in their lives. This interest spurred me to volunteer as a children's teacher in my local church.

My interest in teaching children developed into a passion and led me to pursue a Bachelors degree in Early Childhood Education Studies and a Masters in Social Work. While I have been privileged to teach God's Word to children from 18 months old to 18 years old within the church environment, one thing that was common with several children that I taught was that they struggled to express their thoughts to God in words. After 18 years of teaching children, I had a nudge from the Holy Spirit to write this prayer book. God said that He would like children to connect with Him so that they could build a relationship with Him.

I pray this prayer book helps you draw closer to God in Jesus' name.

Funke Ogunoiki

Never stop praying (*Pray without ceasing*)

1 Thessalonians 5:17

Talking to God

Do you know that in the Bible, Jesus' disciples asked Him to teach them how to pray? Jesus was so happy to teach them how to pray, He taught them "The Lord's Prayer." I want you to know that it is perfectly okay for you to learn how to pray. I have used The Lord's Prayer that Jesus taught the disciples to come up with prayers that you can pray to God at any time and anywhere of your choice.

God would like to listen to your voice every day as He wants to spend time with you. Also, God would like to talk to you as He loves connecting with every one of His children worldwide. Isn't that amazing?

In this book, you will find prayers that are grouped under themes such as; The Lord's Prayer, morning and night prayers, thanksgiving prayers, prayers about your feelings, prayers for the world, prayers before you eat, and many more.

I added Bible verses at the beginning of each theme of prayers as they make our prayers to be powerful as Bible verses are the truths of God's Word. You could learn the Bible verses by memorising them.

Finally, you could say the prayers on your own, or read them with your parents or carers, at any time and in any situation. The most important thing is for you to stay connected to God every day and throughout your day.

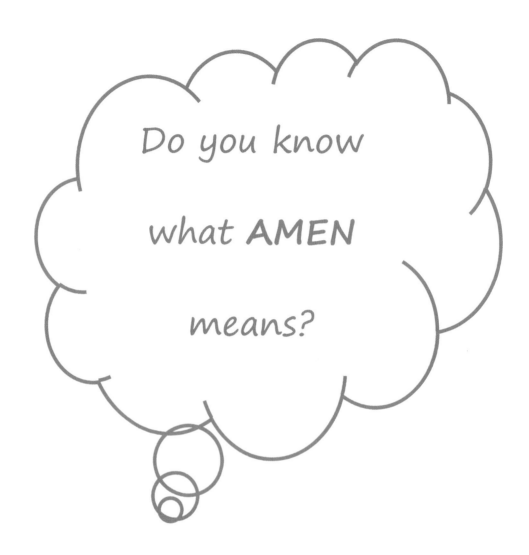

Do you know what **AMEN** means?

Amen means this is true. So when you say Amen at the end of your prayer, you are reminding yourself that "*I really believe what I said is true, I really mean this, and I want my prayers to be answered.*"

Let me share 2 interesting facts about **AMEN**

The 1ˢᵗ interesting fact is: In the Book of Revelation 3:14, God was called: **The Amen, the Faithful and the True Witness. Isn't it amazing that God's name is Amen?**

The 2ⁿᵈ interesting fact is: When Jesus taught the disciples how to pray, he ended his prayers by saying "Amen."

The Lord's Prayer

In this manner, therefore, pray

Matthew 6:9-13

Our Father in heaven,

Hallowed be Your name,

Your kingdom come,

Your will be done,

On earth, as it is in heaven.

Give us this day our daily bread,

And forgive us our debts,

As we forgive our debtors,

And do not lead us into temptation,

But deliver us from the evil one,

For Yours is the kingdom and the power and the glory forever,

Amen.

Praising God

I will praise You, Lord my God, with all my heart

Psalm 86:12

1. Blessed be the name of the Lord,

Who lives forevermore,

Who reigns forevermore.

2. Holy, Holy, Holy,

Lord God Almighty,

Early in the morning,

Our songs shall rise to thee.

3. Lord,

You are Righteous,

You are Holy,

You are Precious.

4. What a Beautiful God You are,

What a Powerful God You are,

What a Mighty God You are.

5. O Lord,

Your works are wonderful and beautiful,

You are a wonderful God,

You are a Great God,

I love You!

6. How Great is my God,

My God is strong and mighty,

He created the heavens and the earth,

My God is All-Powerful.

I will thank God

Be thankful to Him, and bless His name

Psalm 100:4

7. Thank You, God, for loving me,

Thank You, God, for caring about me,

I love You.

8. Thank You, God, for Your peace,

Thank You, God, for Your joy,

Thank You, God, for Your love.

9. Thank You, God, for Your faithfulness,

Thank You, God, for Your kindness,

Thank You, God, for Your gentleness and patience.

10. Thank You, God, that I can smile,

Thank You, God, that I can sleep, jump, play and eat.

11. Thank You, God, for creating me,

Thank You, God, for creating my family,

Thank You, God, for knowing all about me.

12. Thank You, God, for my home,

Thank You, God, for my bed,

Thank You, God, for everything that You are providing for me,

I love You!

13. Thank You, Jesus, for creating animals,

Thank You for all the beautiful plants,

Thank You for all the pets that we have around us.

14. Thank You, God, for all that You are doing for me,

Thank You, God, for your good plans for my life,

Plans to prosper me,

Plans to give me hope and a future,

In Jesus' name,

Amen.

15. Dear God,

Thank You for always providing for my family.

You are awesome!

You are the best!

16. Thank You, God, for my school,

Thank You for all my teachers,

Thank You for everyone at my school.

In the Morning

My voice You shall hear in the morning, O Lord

Psalm 5:3a

17. Dear God,

Thank You for a good night rest,

Thank You for rest and shelter of the night,

Thank you for a new morning,

Please, be with me today,

In Jesus' name,

Amen.

18.   Dear God,
I commit today into Your hands,
Lord, guide me,
Help me in all that I do,
In Jesus' name,
Amen.

19.   Dear Lord,
Come into my heart today,
Come into my heart to stay,
Come into my heart Lord,
In Jesus' name,
Amen.

20.   Good morning Father,
Good morning Jesus,
Good morning Holy Spirit.

21.   Father God,
Thank You for a new morning,
Lord, be with me today,
In Jesus' name,
Amen.

22.   Dear Lord,

Into Your hands, I commit today,

Please, look after me today,

Bless me,

In Jesus' name,

Amen.

23.   Dear Lord,

Thank You for a new day,

Thank You for protecting me,

Thank You for sound sleep,

In Jesus' name,

Amen.

24.   Dear Lord,

Help me to spend today with a smile on my face,

In Jesus' name,

Amen.

25.   Dear Lord,

Thank You for sleeping and waking up,

Lord, please, help me to spend today with Your love in my heart,

In Jesus' name,

Amen.

26.   Dear Lord,

Thank You for sleeping and waking up,

Lord, please help me to spend today with Your joy in my heart,

In Jesus' name,

Amen.

27. Dear Lord,

Thank You for sleeping and waking up,

Lord, please help me to spend today with Your peace in my heart,

In Jesus' name,

Amen.

28. Dear Lord,

Thank You for a good night rest,

Please, help me to have my thinking cap on all day today,

In Jesus' name,

Amen.

29. Dear Lord,

Thank You for a good night rest,

Please, be with me throughout today,

In Jesus' name,

Amen.

30. Dear Lord, throughout today

Help and direct my day,

Fill me with Your love today,

In Jesus' name,

Amen.

31. Dear Lord,

As I start today,

Please, guide and lead me,

Watch over me,

In Jesus' name,

Amen.

On my Bed

When I remember You on my bed, I think of you

Psalm 63:6

32.   Dear God,

It's time to sleep,

Please, protect me as I snuggle in my bed,

In Jesus' name,

Amen.

33. Dear Lord,

The night has come,

It's time to sleep,

Please, watch over me as I sleep,

Keep me safe,

In Jesus' name,

Amen.

34. Dear Lord,

I would like to thank You for today,

Thank you for watching over me throughout the day,

Thank You for the food I ate,

Thank You for all the fun I had,

Thank God, You're the best!

35. Dear Lord,

Thank You for all that happened today,

Thank You, God, for all that I have learned today,

Please, grant me sound sleep,

Please, watch over me as I sleep,

In Jesus' name,

Amen.

Forgiveness

When we do something wrong, it is called sin and when we sin we need to say sorry to Jesus which means forgiveness. When we ask Jesus to forgive us, He will wash away our sins and makes our hearts clean (You can read more about this in 1 John 1:9)

36. Dear God,

Thank You for sending Jesus to die on the cross so that we can have our sins forgiven,

Thank You for forgiving my sins,

Please, help me to forgive others as You forgive us,

In Jesus' name,

Amen.

37. Dear God,

I am sorry I did _____.

Will You please forgive me?

In Jesus' name,

Amen.

Food (Prayers before You Eat)

God gives food to every creature

Psalm 136:25

38. Dear Lord,

I present my food to You,

Please, bless my food,

In Jesus' name,

Amen.

39. Dear Lord,

Please, bless my food,

Provide for those that do not have any food to eat,

In Jesus' name,

Amen.

40. Dear Lord,

Thank You for my food and drink,

Please, let this food nourish my body,

In Jesus' name,

Amen.

My Feelings

Be strong and courageous. Do not be afraid, for the Lord your God will be with you

Joshua 1:9

41.   Dear God,

I know when I'm scared or worried about anything,

I can talk to You and I believe You will hear me,

Thank You, Lord.

42.   Dear God,

Please take away my worries,

am sometimes worried about (*mention what you are worried about to God*).

43. Dear God,

Please help me when I'm sad,

Help me to be joyful even when some things are making me sad,

In Jesus' name,

Amen

44. Dear God,

Please, help me to be strong and brave whenever I am afraid,

In Jesus' name,

Amen

45. Dear Lord,

I feel like crying,

I don't feel well,

Lord, be with me,

Heal me,

In Jesus' name,

Amen.

I will be Outstanding

Then this Daniel distinguished himself above the governors and satraps, because an excellent spirit was in him

Daniel 6:3

OUTSTANDING

GOOD

AVERAGE

46. Dear Lord,

Help me to be outstanding in my school work,

Help me to be outstanding in my character and in all that I do,

In Jesus' name,

Amen.

47. O Lord,

Please, make me wiser than my years,

Let Your Spirit of wisdom guide me,

In Jesus' name,

Amen.

48. Father God,

I will be great in life,

I will be outstanding,

In Jesus' name,

Amen.

My Birthday

This is the day that the Lord has made; We will rejoice and be glad in it

Psalm 118: 24

49. Father God,

Today, I am (insert your age),

Thank You, God, for keeping me alive to see another year,

Thank You for watching over me,

Please, help me to have a happy day,

In Jesus' name,

Amen.

50.   Dear Lord,

Help me to be who You want me to be in life,

In Jesus' name,

Amen.

51.   Dear Lord,

Thank You for the fun that I had today,

Thank You for providing for my mummy and daddy,

Thank You for other children in the world who were born today,

In Jesus' name,

Amen.

Back to School Prayers

Commit your works to the Lord, And your thoughts will be established

Proverbs 16:3

52. Father God,

As I start this new school year,

Please, help me to focus at school,

In Jesus' name,

Amen.

53.   Father God,

As I start this new school year,

Help me to be outstanding in my school work,

In Jesus' name,

Amen.

54.   Father God,

Please, grant me a teachable heart,

To learn well at school,

In Jesus' name,

Amen.

55.   Father God,

Grant me wisdom and knowledge,

In this new school term,

In Jesus' name,

Amen.

56.   Father God,

Watch over me during this school year,

Please, keep me safe,

In Jesus' name,

Amen.

End of School Term Prayers

The Helper, the Holy Spirit, whom the Father will send in Jesus' name, He will teach you all things

John 14:26

57. Father God,

Thank You for helping me throughout this term,

Thank You for the opportunity to learn,

I appreciate your help.

58. Dear Lord,

Thank You for my school,

Thank You for the fun I have had with friends,

Thank You for my teachers.

59. Father God,

Please, watch over me during this holiday season,

Watch over my family and friends,

In Jesus' name,

Amen.

60. Dear Lord,

The holiday is coming,

It's time to rest and refresh,

Lord, help me to enjoy my holiday,

Protect me over the holiday period,

In Jesus' name,

Amen.

Lord, Protect Me

For the LORD your God is the one who goes with you

Deuteronomy 20:4

61. Dear God,

Help me to be at the right place at the right time,

Keep me safe in your arms,

In Jesus' name,

Amen.

62. O Lord,

Please watch over me,

Keep me safe in Your arms,

In Jesus' name,

Amen.

63. Dear Lord,

Will You protect and guide my mind?

Direct my thought in ways that will make You happy,

In Jesus' name,

Amen.

64. Dear Lord,

Fill me with Your wisdom and understanding,

In Jesus' name,

Amen.

65. Christ be with my going out,

Christ be in my speaking,

Christ be with me at all times,

In Jesus' name,

Amen.

66. Christ be with my Mum and Dad,

Christ be with me at school,

Christ be with my going out and coming in,

Christ be with my friends,

In Jesus' name,

Amen.

67. Christ be with my cousins,

Christ be with my uncles and aunties,

Christ be with my grandparents,

In Jesus' name,

Amen.

68.   Dear Lord,

Please, keep me from all evil,

Keep my life in Your hands,

In Jesus' name,

Amen.

69.   O Lord,

Will You look after everyone in my family?

Watch over us,

Protect us from danger,

In Jesus' name,

Amen.

The Weather

For He (God) says to the snow, 'Fall on the earth'

Job 37:6

70. Thank You, God, for the winter season,

Thank You, God, for the autumn season,

Thank You, God, for the summer season,

Thank You, God, for the spring season,

In Jesus' name,

Amen.

71.   I Praise You, Lord, for the beauty of the winter,

I Praise You, Lord, for the beauty of all the seasons,

In Jesus' name,

Amen.

72.   Thank You, God, for sending rain on the earth,

Thank You, God, for the beautiful sunshine,

Thank You, God, for the wind,

In Jesus' name,

Amen.

My Church

I will build my church

Matthew 16:18

73. Dear Lord,

Thank You for my church,

Thank You for every Christian in the world,

Thank You for watching over us,

In Jesus' name,

Amen.

74. Dear Lord,

Let Your peace and love be with my church friends,

In Jesus' name,

Amen.

75. Dear Lord,

Please help my friends and I to put Your Word into practice,

In Jesus' name,

Amen.

The World

In the beginning, God created the heavens and the earth

Genesis 1:1

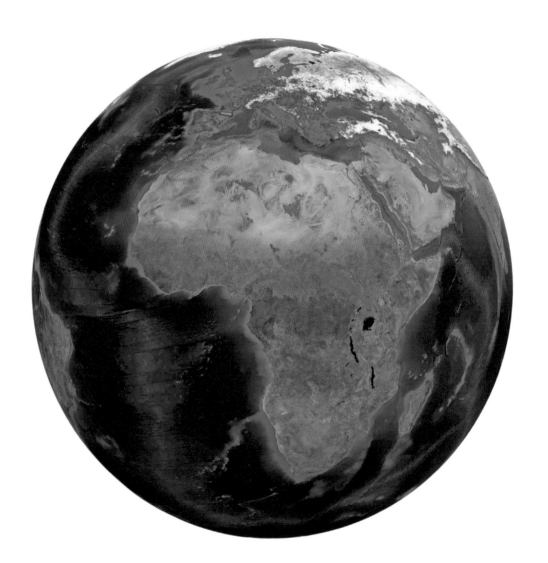

76. Father God,

Thank You for having the whole world under your control,

Thank You for having the whole world in Your hands,

In Jesus' name,

Amen.

77. Dear Lord,

I Praise You, O God, for the whole world,

For the birds,

For the trees and plants,

For the animals,

For the wisdom that You have given us,

For the sea,

For the sky,

For all the creatures,

How amazing that you have made this wonderful world,

I love You!

78. Father God,

Will You please shine Your light on the whole world?

Do not allow darkness to dominate the earth,

Let Your light dominates the whole world,

In Jesus' name,

Amen.

79. Father God,

Please, comfort those who are sad in the world,

Help them to know about You

Help them to know You are our hope and strength,

In Jesus' name,

Amen.

Easter

od demonstrates his own love for us in this: While we were still sinners, Christ died for us

Romans 5:8

80. Lord Jesus,

Thank You for your death on the cross,

Thank You for taking the punishment for our sins,

Thank You for conquering death,

Thank You for rising up to life again so that we can all be saved,

I love You Jesus!

81. Dear Lord,

Thank You for Your love for us,

Your love is so deep,

I can't explain it,

I just want to thank You Lord for loving me.

82. Lord Jesus,

Thank You for reminding us that You are coming back again,

Halleluyah!

Christ will come back again!

Christmas

Then the Angel said to them, "Do not be afraid, for behold, I bring you good tidings of great joy which will be to all people. For there is born to you this day in the city of David a Saviour, who is Christ the Lord"

Luke 2:10-11

83. Dear Lord,

It's time to remember You

On this special day,

I am so happy it's Christmas!

84. Dear Lord,

Today is the day Christians have chosen to celebrate Your birthday,

Thank You for coming to the world to save us.

85. Father God,

Thank You for bringing us everlasting hope and joy through the birth of Jesus.

86. Father God,

I pray as we celebrate Christmas today,

Anyone that does not know You,

I pray they will experience Your love and they will connect with You,

In Jesus' name,

Amen.

Christ was Born, Christ is Risen and Christ will come again!

Printed in Great Britain
by Amazon

74649807R00030